The Extraordinary Life of Thomas Peters

by Susannah Flaherty

 HOUGHTON MIFFLIN HARCOURT
School Publishers

ILLUSTRATION CREDIT: **Title Page** Bandelin-Dacey Studios.

PHOTOGRAPHY CREDITS: **Cover** © Peter Harholdt/SuperStock. **2** The Granger Collection, New York. **7** Private Collection, Peter Newark American Pictures/The Bridgeman Art Library. **9** American Museum, Bath, Avon, UK, Courtesy of the Director, National Army Museum, London, UK / The Bridgeman Art Library. **10** The Granger Collection, New York. **11** The Art Archive. **13** © Peter Harholdt/SuperStock, Inc. **15** The Granger Collection, New York. **17** The Granger Collection, New York.

Printed in China

ISBN-13: 978-0-547-01759-4
ISBN-10: 0-547-01759-6

14 15 16 17 0940 19 18 17 16
4500569761

Table of Contents

During the American Revolution, colonial Patriots fought for "life, liberty, and the pursuit of happiness." Their struggle for freedom from the British is well known.

But the Patriots were not the only people yearning for liberty during the Revolution. There was another group of people whose struggle for freedom is largely unknown, even today. Who were those people? They were black Africans and their descendants who were enslaved in the American colonies.

Around 1750, there were about 300,000 enslaved people in the colonies. Most were African. They represented about 20 percent of the total colonial population.

The Slave Trade

European slave-trading companies made thousands of voyages to West Africa to buy African captives. Historians estimate that these companies brought at least 10 to 12 million Africans to a life of slavery in the Americas.

Some enslaved blacks fought with the Patriots during the Revolutionary War. However, historians believe that many more ran away from their colonial masters to join the British or Loyalists.

Why did many enslaved blacks support the British during the Revolutionary War, and what became of them afterward? This selection answers these questions and tells the extraordinary true story of one man—Thomas Peters—who seized his own opportunity for life, liberty, and the pursuit of happiness.

Thomas Peters's Early Life

Thomas Peters was probably born in a region of West Africa that is now a part of Nigeria. Kidnapped as a young man, he was taken to North America and sold into slavery around 1760.

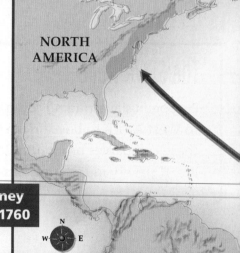

Thomas Peters's journey into slavery, around 1760

NORTH AMERICA

In the early 1770s, Peters was resold to a colonist named William Campbell, who lived on the Cape Fear River in North Carolina. Logging trees and milling them into timber was the local industry; the enslaved Peters was made apprentice to a millwright.

By the end of 1774, tensions between the colonists and the British government had reached a breaking point. War began in the spring of 1775 when the first battles of the Revolutionary War were fought at Lexington and Concord.

Rumors spread among the colonists in North Carolina. Many feared that the British would encourage the enslaved blacks to rise up and revolt against them. Such unrest would make it difficult for the colonists to succeed in their fight against the British.

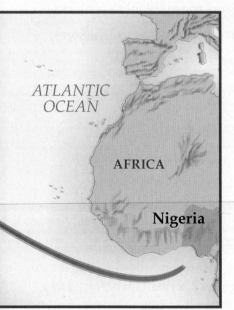

ATLANTIC OCEAN

AFRICA

Nigeria

Promises of Freedom

The colonists' fears were realized in November 1775. Lord Dunmore, the British governor of Virginia and a powerful Loyalist, issued a proclamation that contained a remarkable offer. It promised freedom to any man enslaved by a Patriot, as long as he agreed to fight for the British. (But this offer of freedom did not extend to enslaved people owned by Loyalist colonists.)

News of Lord Dunmore's proclamation quickly spread. Many colonists were outraged. They felt that Lord Dunmore was stealing their "property" and trying to create unrest.

Nevertheless, Lord Dunmore's proclamation had the effect he had hoped for. It inspired many blacks—including Thomas Peters—to escape from their Patriot masters, join British troops, and claim their liberty.

"And I hereby further declare all indentured Servants, Negroes, or others, (appertaining to Rebels,) free that are able and willing to bear Arms, they joining His MAJESTY'S Troops as soon as may be."

In this proclamation, Lord Dunmore offered freedom to Patriot-owned enslaved Africans and indentured servants who ran away and joined British troops.

Black Patriots in the Revolution

Why didn't the Patriots let enslaved black men fight on their side, too? At the start of the Revolutionary War, they did. Black Patriots, both free and enslaved, fought beside other colonists at the battles of Lexington, Concord, and Bunker Hill.

However, later in 1775, General George Washington barred blacks from serving in the Continental Army. The reasons for this decision were complex. Most Patriots did not want to give weapons to the people they had enslaved. They feared that allowing them to fight would lead to uprisings.

As the war continued, the Continental Army desperately needed more soldiers. Because of the American troop shortage, Washington changed his mind. Despite the tentative feelings of many colonists, Washington permitted blacks to enlist.

General George Washington

A Free Man

When Thomas Peters's chance for liberty arrived, he took it. In early 1776, a fleet of British ships sailed up the Cape Fear River. When Peters learned that British forces were so near, he fled from bondage to join them. According to Lord Dunmore's proclamation, he was now a free man.

Peters joined the Black Pioneers, a British military unit composed entirely of black men. The Pioneers did not fight, but they still made major contributions to the Loyalist cause. Some worked as army scouts and raiders. Others were military engineers. They built housing and fortifications for soldiers, sometimes constructing military defenses during battle under dangerous conditions.

The Black Brigade

During the Revolutionary War, British military authorities organized other regiments of formerly enslaved blacks. One of the most famous was the Black Brigade. The Brigade conducted surprise attacks on Patriot forces with great dexterity. They also captured prisoners and seized supplies. Their leader was a black Loyalist known as Colonel Tye.

Peters stayed with the Black Pioneers for the remainder of the war and was promoted to sergeant.

In 1779, the British issued another influential proclamation, known as the Philipsburg Proclamation. Previously, the British had granted freedom to only enslaved men. But the Philipsburg Proclamation expanded the British offer of

British General Henry Clinton issued the Philipsburg Proclamation in 1779.

freedom to include enslaved women and children, too. They had to run away from their colonial masters and reach the British forces. Then they would be free.

Historians believe that sometime after the Philipsburg Proclamation, an enslaved black woman named Sally escaped from her Patriot master and reached a British army camp. At some point, she met Thomas Peters, and the two were married. Later they had children.

The British Are Defeated

In October 1781, George Washington's army defeated the forces of British General Charles Cornwallis at Yorktown, Virginia. It was a major victory for the Americans, effectively ending the Revolutionary War.

At Yorktown, black Loyalist soldiers were among Cornwallis's troops. After Cornwallis and his forces had surrendered, the surviving black soldiers were captured by the Americans and returned to slavery. Unfortunately, many black Loyalists would meet this sad end after the war.

In late 1782, the British signed a provisional peace treaty with the Americans. In it, they recognized their former colonies as an independent nation. After the treaty was signed, the victorious Americans made a demand. They insisted that the departing British troops return all American property that they had taken. Among the "property" the Americans wanted back were the thousands of formerly enslaved people who had joined the British during the war.

The British surrendered at Yorktown.

Escape from Slavery

Black Loyalists were terrified at the thought of being forced back into slavery. A man named Boston King later wrote that he felt "inexpressible anguish and terror... Many of the slaves had very cruel masters, so that the thoughts of returning home with them embittered life to us."

But British commander Sir Guy Carleton would not agree to the American demand. He refused to forsake the black Loyalists. Instead, he arranged for them to leave the colonies permanently. Carleton organized ships to take black Loyalists to places that were controlled by the British. Some were taken to Nova Scotia in Canada or

A medal marking the end of slavery in the British Empire

to Jamaica in the Caribbean. Others went to Great Britain.

Not all black Loyalists were able to take advantage of Carleton's arrangement and leave the country. Many were captured by American forces and returned to slavery. But 3,000 to 4,000 black Loyalists did escape. Thomas Peters and his family were among them. Safely aboard a British ship, the Peters family left the port of New York for Nova Scotia around the beginning of 1783.

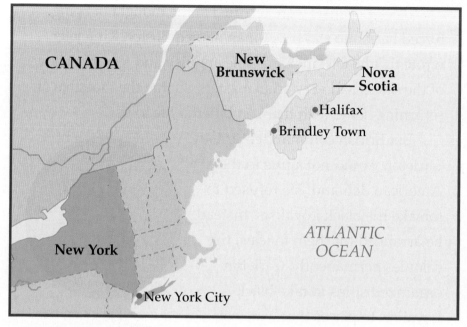

The Peters family sailed from New York to Nova Scotia.

The ship carrying the Peters family was blown off course, and they had to spend the winter in the Caribbean. Finally, they arrived in Nova Scotia, Canada, in 1784. After their arrival in Nova Scotia, the Peters family, along with other black Loyalists, settled in Brindley Town.

All Loyalists—soldiers and formerly enslaved Africans—had been promised 100 acres of farmland, tools, and three years' worth of provisions. But Peters's group of black Loyalists received provisions to last them only a few months. They never received their land grants.

As they waited for their land, Peters and his community were forced to build roads in return for their meager provisions. They were kept apart from the white Loyalists and made to live in desperately poor settlements.

Thomas Peters personally petitioned the governor of Nova Scotia for the group's land grants. His efforts resulted in some black Loyalist families receiving one-acre "town plots." All their attempts to settle on larger farming plots were blocked. The families barely survived.

Again and again, Peters tried to persuade the governor to grant the promised farmlands. All of his efforts were unsuccessful.

Finally, in 1790, Peters decided to travel to Great Britain and petition the British government in person. Hundreds of black Loyalists gave him written permission to legally represent them. He crossed the Atlantic Ocean to London, England. The voyage was risky. While at sea, he could have been captured by pirates and perhaps enslaved again.

Peters sailed to England in 1790.

13

The Sierra Leone Company

After arriving safely in England, Thomas Peters met a man named Granville Sharp. Sharp was a famous anti-slavery activist. With Sharp's help, Peters succeeded in delivering his petition to the British government.

The petition outlined every aspect of the black Loyalists' frustrations. They had not received the land they had been promised. Nor had they received tools or provisions. But that was not all. The black Loyalists also had been denied such British rights as trial by jury, access to courts of law, and the vote.

Granville Sharp offered to help Peters in another way. He told Peters about the Sierra Leone Company. This company had been created by Sharp and other British abolitionists. They wished to create a colony in Sierra Leone, Africa, for formerly enslaved blacks. Their first attempt to establish a colony had failed. Now they were looking for a new group of people willing to rebuild the Sierra Leone settlement.

Peters realized that resettling in Sierra Leone could solve the black Loyalists' problems. He agreed to Granville Sharp's proposal.

With Peters's agreement, Sharp and the Sierra Leone Company presented a new plan to the British government. The plan proposed to resettle Peters and the black Loyalists in Sierra Leone.

The British anti-slavery movement continued to grow. This painting shows an abolitionist meeting in London in 1840.

The British government agreed to pay the costs of transporting the Loyalists from Nova Scotia to Sierra Leone. Free passage and 20 acres of land—with added acres for family members—were promised to those who were willing to relocate. After the plan had been approved, Thomas Peters left England and returned to Nova Scotia.

Peters spread the news of the Sierra Leone plan throughout the black Loyalist community. "Free Settlement on the Coast of Africa," proclaimed the company flyer. Frustrated with their current situation in Nova Scotia, many black Loyalists embraced the plan to resettle in Sierra Leone.

Passage to Africa—and Freedom

The Sierra Leone Company had expected only a few hundred black Loyalists to express interest in their offer. They were wrong. Nearly 1,200 people responded.

Thomas Peters helped organize the hundreds of families who signed up for passage to Sierra Leone. By the end of 1791, a fleet of ships sat in the Halifax harbor, ready for the trip to West Africa.

On January 15, 1792, the Peters family and the other black Loyalists set sail for Africa. After weeks of raging storms, the entire fleet arrived safely at their destination in early March. They were free, and their new lives lay ahead.

Peters and the Loyalists immediately began clearing land for their new settlement. With hope in their hearts, they named their new home Freetown.

The Death of Thomas Peters

Tragically, Thomas Peters did not live long after arriving in Sierra Leone. He died of malaria on June 25, 1792. But his legacy remains. The founding of Freetown was a historic moment in black history, and its mission to provide freedom, equal rights, and land to formerly enslaved people was a step toward ending slavery.

The settlers faced many challenges in Sierra Leone. However, their situation improved after Great Britain outlawed the slave trade in 1807. Freetown became a key base for fighting the slave trade and resettling formerly enslaved people. Freetown eventually became the capital of Sierra Leone. Descendants of the original settlers still live there today.

Conclusion

The story of Thomas Peters and the black Loyalists is an extraordinary one, starting with slavery in America and ending with freedom in Sierra Leone. Their experiences may not be widely known, but they are an important part of American Revolutionary War history.

The British attacked a Spanish slave-trading center in Sierra Leone.

Finding themselves in the midst of the struggle between the British and the colonial Patriots, enslaved blacks like Thomas Peters seized the opportunity to gain their own freedom. Their efforts represent one of the largest rebellions of enslaved people in American history.

The Life of Thomas Peters

Pre-1760	Thomas Peters is born in West Africa.
About 1760	Peters is sold into slavery in the American colonies.
Fall 1775	Lord Dunmore's Proclamation is made.
Early 1776	Peters escapes from slavery and joins the Black Pioneers.
June 1779	The Philipsburg Proclamation is made.
Fall 1781	The British surrender at Yorktown.
1782–1783	The British arrange for many black Loyalists to leave the U.S. and travel to Nova Scotia, Jamaica, or Great Britain.
1784	The Peters family arrives in Nova Scotia, but living conditions are poor.
1790	Peters travels to England and meets Granville Sharp of the Sierra Leone Company.
January 1792	Peters sails to Sierra Leone, Africa. He helps establish Freetown with other black Loyalists.
June 1792	Peters dies of malaria in Freetown.

Responding

✔ **TARGET SKILL** **Sequence of Events** What events led up to Thomas Peters joining the Black Pioneers? Copy and complete the chart below, adding boxes if necessary.

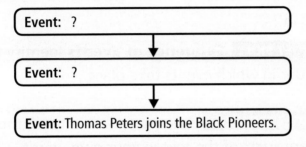

Event: ?

↓

Event: ?

↓

Event: Thomas Peters joins the Black Pioneers.

✏ Write About It

Text to World Peters went to England to ask the British government to protect the black Loyalists' rights. Think about actions people can take today to try to protect their rights. Write a few paragraphs explaining what people can do.

apprentice	dexterity
aspects	influential
authorities	persuade
bondage	provisions
contributions	tentative

✔ **TARGET SKILL** **Sequence of Events** Identify the time order in which events take place.

✔ **TARGET STRATEGY** **Summarize** Briefly tell the important parts of the text in your own words.

GENRE **Narrative Nonfiction** gives factual information by telling a true story.